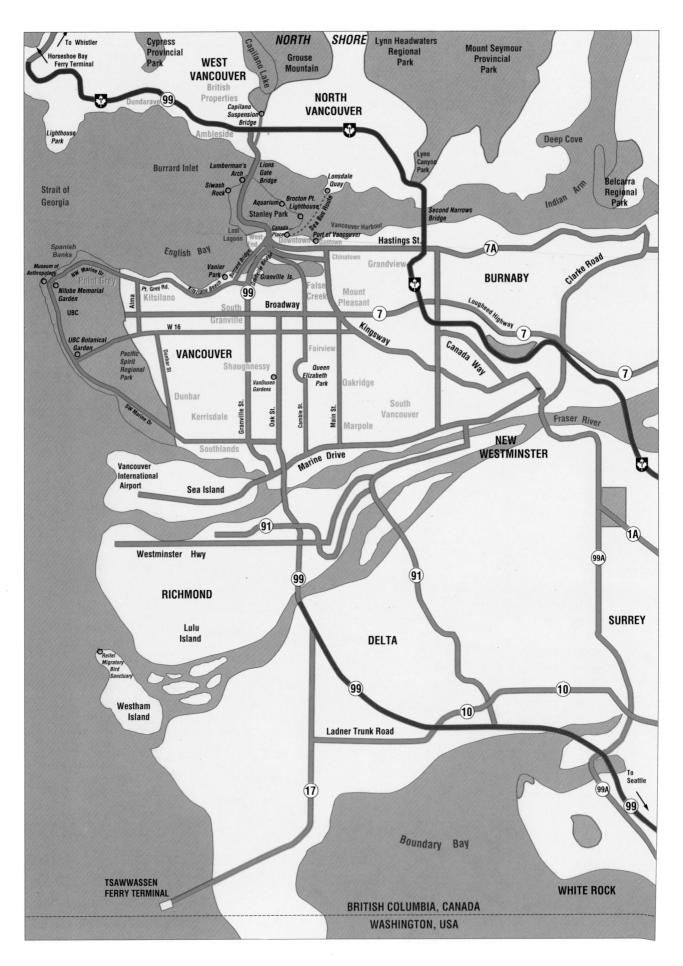

A Portrait of
Vancouver

Vancouver is a delightful city for visitors of all ages.

Contents

Introduction

Vancouver is one of the world's most scenic and most livable cities. There is always plenty to see and enjoy. Large enough to offer a wealth of diversions, it is also small enough for visitors to soon feel at home.

Here in Vancouver, locals share smiles and conversation with strangers. Walking is a joy in this city by the sea, and dozens of parks and gardens offer the opportunity for a leisurely stroll or a demanding mountainside hike. From opera to sporting events, international dining to pizza on the go, and fine art to souvenir postcards, Vancouver combines the best of all worlds.

Although Vancouver is a relatively new city, established in 1886, aboriginal habitation along the forest-shrouded coast dates back 6000 to 8000 years. For centuries, Native people harvested salmon and shellfish and carved totem poles, masks, and other works of art out of cedar. In 1858, the Fraser River Gold Rush lured thousands of American, Chinese and European fortune hunters into the region. After the gold rush was over, the newcomers began logging, fishing, and mining.

From its origins as a remote logging town, the "Village on the Edge of the Rain Forest" has grown into a sparkling metropolis. Gone are the smelters and factories that once darkened the air above False Creek and English Bay. In their place, Granville Island, the West End, Kitsilano, and Robson Street, reflect a distinctively West Coast style.

Opposite *A bird's-eye view of Vancouver.*
Above *Totem poles reflect the city's aboriginal heritage.*

The Harbour

ew cities can boast the wealth of natural beauty that has made Vancouver famous throughout the world. Surrounded by sparkling waters, downtown high rises take on a magical air, rising above the bustle of city streets to offer unparalleled views.

In the midst of it all, Vancouver Harbour is Canada's gateway to the world. The Port of Vancouver, one of the finest year-round service ports anywhere, is also Canada's busiest. Here trade is carried out with 90 nations. More than half of all cargo handled at the port is destined for Pacific Rim countries, such as Japan, South Korea, and China.

From the deck of the spacious pedestrian walkway along Canada Place, Burrard Inlet's Inner Harbour is in full view. Abuzz with

activity, the waterway is shared by Canadian and international vessels, while overhead, light commuter planes and helicopters come and go from destinations along the coast. Beyond Stanley Park's Prospect Point, a dozen or more deepwater vessels await their turn to load or unload.

Rain or shine, the SeaBus, a double-ended catamaran, departs from nearby Waterfront Station for the North Shore's Lonsdale Quay. Built of lightweight aluminum, the SeaBus can turn, as well as stop, in its own length. Either end can become bow or stern at will.

Built for the opening of Expo 86, the five Teflon-coated sails of Canada Place are as distinctive a landmark as Sydney's opera house. Designed to suggest the city's nautical past, the sails cover three city blocks. Enjoy a stroll along

the Canada Place Public Promenades and climb the Harbour Observation Deck for a fine view of Burrard Inlet.

More than 220 luxury cruise ships in all dock here annually, just a few steps away from Vancouver's busiest and most elegant shopping centres. Some 500,000 passengers disembark every year as they stop over enroute to Alaska.

Canada Place is home to the Vancouver Trade and Convention Centre and the Vancouver Board of Trade. The complex also houses a major hotel, restaurants, shops, and art galleries.

__Opposite__ The five sails of Canada Place are a distinctive landmark of Vancouver Harbour. __Above__ Built for Expo 86, Canada Place offers a front-row-centre view of the harbour. __Bottom__ Cruise ships dock within walking distance of downtown shops.

Opposite Canada Day, July 1, celebrated at the Vancouver Trade and Convention Centre. ***Above*** A cruise ship hugs the terminal at Canada Place. ***Bottom*** The view from North Vancouver's Lonsdale Quay across Burrard Inlet to Vancouver city centre.

City lights add sparkle to one of the world's most beautiful horizons. In the distance, the Lions Gate Bridge links Vancouver and the North Shore.

Downtown

Reflecting Vancouver's eclectic nature, downtown streets are filled with eye-catching contrasts. Pedestrians in formal business attire match strides with sports buffs in shorts and runners. Street vendors flog their wares at busy intersections where chess players are absorbed in avid—and very public—competition. Luxury automobiles park alongside dust-covered four-by-four recreational vehicles.

With a population of over 500,000, the city of Vancouver is the hub of the Lower Mainland. Every day, a goodly portion of the regions' 1.5 million people commute into the downtown core—by car, bus, bicycle, SeaBus, and SkyTrain, the areas' fast light-rapid-transit system. Transportation is varied and efficient, putting the city's nooks and crannies within easy reach.

Growth is visible in the busy streets and along the skyline, which seems to change daily. New buildings, both residential and commercial, continue to spring up, joining landmarks such as the Vancouver Art Gallery and the Vancouver Law Courts. A new central library, built on the theme of a Roman coliseum, is just steps away from Pacific Centre, an immense three-level shopping mall at Georgia and Howe Streets.

Nearby is the Robson Square Complex, with its sunken plaza, Media Centre, theatre, and conference centre. Surrounded by major department stores, boutiques, restaurants, coffee shops, book stores and music stores, the square provides a welcome open space in the heart of the city.

The Vancouver Art Gallery, the city's largest, is housed in the former Vancouver Courthouse. Graced with marble walls, columns, and steps, as well as a distinctive central interior rotunda topped with a copper-sheathed dome, the gallery contains four levels displaying Canadian and international artists. Of special note is a permanent exhibition of the artwork of painter and writer Emily Carr, who captured the brooding presence of the West Coast rain forests in her distinctive works.

*Opposite Robson Square is a place for dining and dallying. **Above** Bird of Spring, a sculpture by Inuit artist Abraham Etungat, adds flare to the north end of Robson Square. **Bottom** The main entry to the Great Hall of the Vancouver Law Courts.*

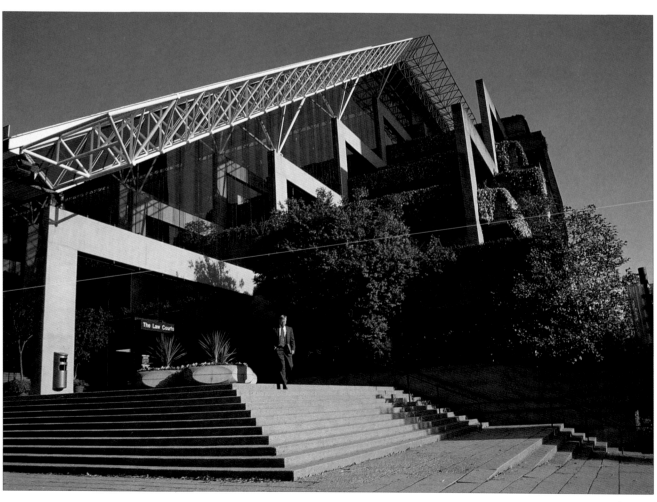

Vancouver is traversed by bridges. The Cambie Street Bridge was rebuilt for Expo 86; others, such as the Granville Street Bridge, Burrard Street Bridge, and Lions Gate Bridge, owe their existence to earlier, more genteel eras.

At night, the Lions Gate Bridge is illuminated by thousands of bright lights. Built in 1937 by the Guinness family, the bridge crosses the First Narrows from Stanley Park to the North

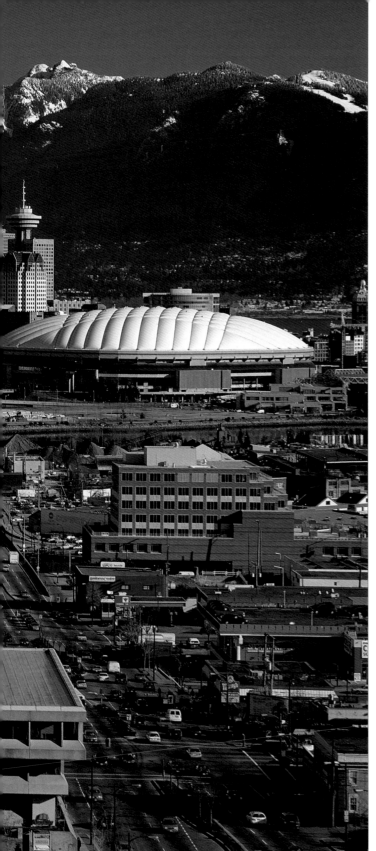

Shore. The construction of this bridge, which was originally a toll bridge, was an architectural triumph. When it was built, the 450-metre-structure was one of the longest suspension bridges in the world.

Opposite *The twin peaks of the Lions are clearly visible on the left in this view along Cambie Street.* **Above** *Stone lions guard the entrance to the Lions Gate Bridge.* **Bottom** *Spanning the First Narrows, the Lions Gate Bridge was built in 1937.*

15

Opposite *Science World's gleaming dome is mirrored in the waters of False Creek.*
Above *Boaters benefit from harbour police protection.*

Vancouver and the sea are inseparable. Foreign visitors came by way of the Pacific Ocean, which touches Vancouver's western boundary as the Strait of Georgia. Spanish explorers such as Don Juan Pantoja y Arriaga and Don José Maria Narvaez visited in

the late 1700s. When Captain George Vancouver, for whom the city is named, arrived in 1792, he discovered that the Spanish had charted the coast the previous year.

On the doorstep of downtown Vancouver, False Creek's meandering waters provide a sparkling backdrop for attractions such as Science World, BC Place Stadium, and Granville Island. Once the site of Expo 86, the north shore of False Creek is being transformed into a new high-rise neighbourhood.

Robson Street

Robson Street begins at BC Place Stadium and heads west to its conclusion at Stanley Park's Lost Lagoon. Although it extends a mere 19 blocks, the influence of Robson Street has always been great. No thoroughfare better sums up what Vancouver is all about.

Famed for its Old World German restaurants and delicatessens, Robson was once known locally as Robsonstrasse. Today it has an international flavour, with evidence of European, Asian, and U.S. influences.

Fashion is the essence of Robson Street. Clothing, shoes, accessories—whether purchased in boutiques and gallerias or at larger stores like Eaton's—draw visitors of all ages. The world's leading designers, including Chanel, Cartier, and Ferragamo, have opened exquisite

shops here. Canadian designers, as well, are represented in the wide selection of all things wearable.

Mingling with the clothing stores are restaurants to suit every taste. Japanese sushi, Asian curries, Mexican burritos, vegetarian gourmet specialties, bagels, pizzas, and Canadian standbys can all be sampled here. Like Vancouver itself, Robson Street encompasses a barrage of cultures, combining to create a vital, colourful ambience.

Walking east along "the Robson Strip" past Granville Street, one of the newest areas of city development opens up. The $100-million Vancouver Public Library, the $24.5 million Ford Theatre, presenting the latest theatrical spectacles, and the $160-million General Motors Place sports stadium are a threesome that is turning a

formerly quiet corner of Robson Street into a cultural enclave. Complete with shops, restaurants, and cafés, Robson East is also adjacent to BC Place and the Queen Elizabeth Theatre complex.

Going west along Robson Street, it's a short walk through the West End to English Bay or Stanley Park. Along the way, pass through Barclay Heritage Square Park, where nine historic turn-of-the-century houses have been refurbished to their former glory. With their well-tended gardens, they are a reminder of the West End's genteel origin as home to the rich and powerful.

***Opposite** Since the 1960s, a profusion of high rises has sprung up in the West End. **Above** Casual and sporty, Vancouver is a fitness buff's paradise. **Bottom** Robson Street is alive with cafés, boutiques, and souvenir shops.*

Gastown

The year 1867 marked a real first for the future city of Vancouver: Gassy Jack Deighton arrived on the south shore of Burrard Inlet. Accompanied by his Native wife and a barrel of whisky, the talkative Mr. Deighton convinced the locals to build him a saloon. Twenty-four hours later, Gastown was born.

Within three years, the ramshackle community of sawmills, loggers' cabins, and drinking halls built on the edge of the rain forest was renamed Granville. The name didn't stick: in April of 1886, the City of Vancouver was officially incorporated.

Renovation and refurbishment of its many warehouses has polished Gastown's tarnished, yet intriguing, image. Today its turn-of-the-century architecture, cobblestone streets, and old-fashioned lampposts suggest a more illustrious past.

Gastown's most memorable landmark is located at the corner of Cambie and Water Streets. Based on an 1875 design, the Gastown steam clock is the only steam-operated clock in the world. Every hour on the hour, clouds of vapour from an underground system steam out of the clock's top, accompanied by the sounds of the Westminster chimes.

Opposite The steam clock is a treasured Gastown landmark. *Above* Cobblestone streets add Old World ambience to Gastown, Vancouver's oldest quarter.

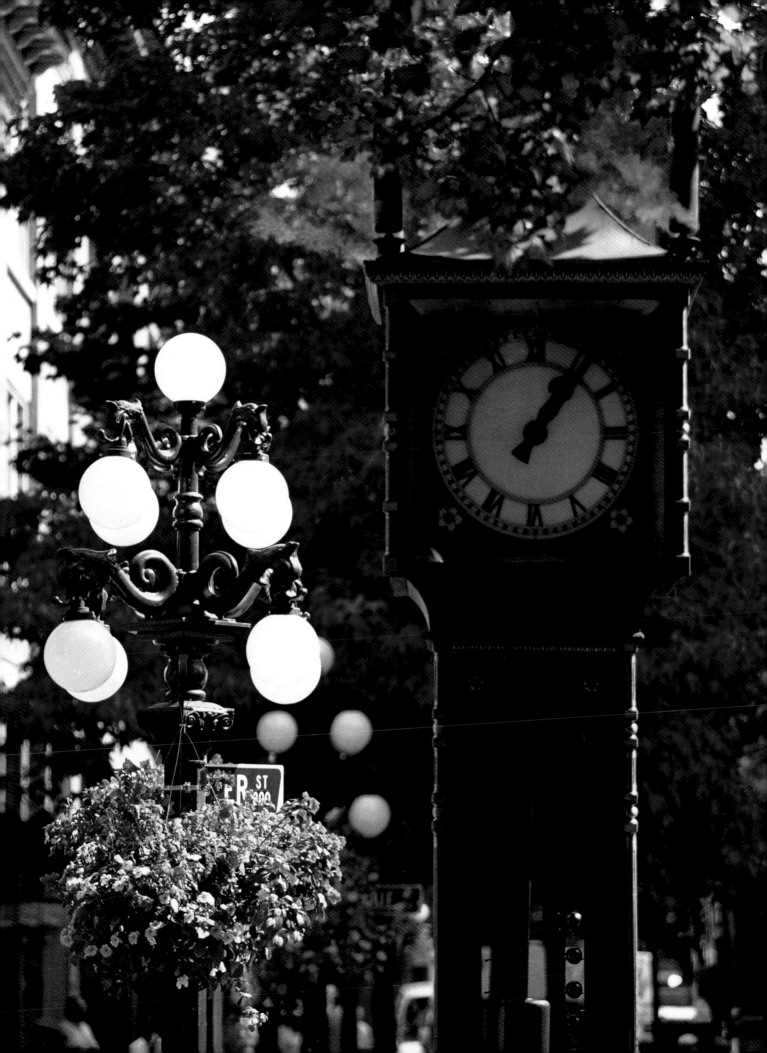

Chinatown

Hustle and bustle is the essence of Chinatown, one of the Vancouver's earliest developed communities. Up and down the streets of this busy historic area, vendors ply their wares to passersby. Stands piled high with fruits and vegetables spill out onto the sidewalk. Inside the nonfood shops of Chinatown you'll find rattan furniture and paper lanterns, Chinese kitchen utensils, and embroidered silk blouses. Browsing is encouraged.

The first Chinese immigrants to British Columbia came during the Fraser gold rush of the 1850s. Many settled in Victoria or New Westminster. In 1880, the Canadian Pacific Railway (CPR) began to use Chinese labourers to blast the lines through Western Canada. Thousands died completing the dangerous work of building the transcontinental railway.

Architecturally, Chinatown has maintained some of Vancouver's oldest buildings. The Sam Kee Building at 8 West Pender Street, is the narrowest commercial building in the world. Nearby is the Chinese Cultural Centre, established in 1973. Marking the entrance is the colourful Pavilion Gate, donated by the Chinese government after Expo 86. To the rear of the centre is the Dr. Sun Yat-Sen Classical Chinese Garden. As the only authentic classical garden ever constructed outside China, it is a singular example of a Ming Dynasty garden.

Opposite Originally a part of the Chinese Pavilion at Expo 86, this eye-catching gate is now a Chinatown attraction. *Above* The Dr. Sun Yat Sen Classical Chinese Garden is an oasis of tranquillity.

Granville Island

One of the liveliest of Vancouver attractions, False Creek's Granville Island is a relative newcomer to the city. A crowded, polluted industrial site since 1916, the island gained a new lease on life in the 1970s. The lumber mills, smelters, barges, and shantytown were replaced by the spacious Granville Island Market, as well as restaurants, theatres, an art school, marina facilities, dozens of shops, and a creekside hotel.

The rehabilitated and renovated Granville Island opened for business on July 12, 1979. It was an overnight success and has remained a success ever since. Every year its popularity seems to increase. More than 90,000 people now visit the island annually.

Who would have thought that this once smoky, smelly site of pioneer industries would ever be transformed? But once under way, Granville Island could not be stopped. Its influence has spread to nearby Fairview Slopes, where a community of condominium dwellers has sprung up. In addition, a pedestrian walkway now forms a link between Kitsilano Beach and Stanley Park by way of BC Place, one of the last vestiges of Expo 86.

Opposite The Granville Island Public Market is a cornucopia of sights, smells, and tastes. ***Above*** All aboard the Granville Island mini-ferry service.

I n any season, the Granville Island Public Market offers a bounty of fresh local and imported produce and baked goods. Choose from oven-baked goods and confections, meats and seafood, fruits and vegetables, seasonal and dried flowers, deli and specialty foods, and wines.

As you'll discover, the market offers more than eatables and drinkables—it's a treasure trove of hand-crafted wares created by local artisans. Pottery, glass, woodworking, and fine jewellery, can all be purchased here.

There's more than enough on Granville Island to delight any child. Overlooking False Creek, the island is home to bobbing boats and friendly sea gulls. Catch a mini-ferry for a round trip across False Creek. The island is a favoured location for magicians, face painters, musicians, clowns, and jugglers, who perform year-round for children and adults alike.

Another lively attraction is the Kids Only Market. Located just inside the entrance to the island, this market is a complex of children's boutiques, with thousands of toys on display. Just a few steps away is a zany water park with inviting slides and sprinklers.

*Opposite A juggler on Granville Island entertains shoppers with skillful feats. **Above** Children enjoy the island's playgrounds, bicycle paths, and Kids Only Market. **Bottom** Street performers include clowns, magicians, and musicians.*

29

Down on Granville Island, behind the famed Emily Carr College of Art and Design, is Sea Village, one of the city's last houseboat communities. These nautical residences capture the essence of the West Coast lifestyle.

Above right A pedestrian walkway curves passed Granville Island's Maritime Market.
Above left False Creek, spanned by the Burrard Street Bridge. *Bottom* Sea Village floating homes moored at Granville Island.

False Creek residences overlook pedestrians, joggers, and bicyclists, as well as the occasional dragon boat. Competition is fierce during the summer's annual Dragon Boat Festival, and paddlers start training early.

Walking along the False Creek seawall is a pleasure. Meandering east and west of Granville Island, the seawall skirts marinas where small craft are moored on the protective inland waters.

Stanley Park

More than a century ago, Vancouver's first city council dreamed of a magnificent park in the midst of a thriving metropolis. At the time, the city was no more than a few cabins huddled together. The proposed park was a good hike from homes and industry at the site of a Squamish summer village named Khwaykhway, which had been designated a military reserve by the Canadian government in case of U.S. attack.

On September 27, 1889, Stanley Park was born, named after Lord Stanley, then Governor General of Canada. At the formal dedication, Lord Stanley proclaimed his famous decree. The park, he affirmed, was "for the use and enjoyment of peoples of all colours, creeds and customes, for all time." It has remained that way to this day.

One of the many highlights of the park is Brockton Point, with its eight totem poles. The first totems were brought to Stanley Park in the 1920s. Original poles have since been replicated or replaced with newer sculptures.

Representing the works of North and South Kwakiutl, Haida, Nuu-chah-nulth, and Nishga artists, the poles are now clustered in the lower Brockton area. Images on the poles include Thunderbird, with its wings outstretched, and Raven, with its extended beak, as well as Wolf, Beaver, Eagle, and Whale.

Opposite The first totem poles were raised at Brockton Point in 1924.
Above *Westeria-draped Stanley Park Dining Pavilion.*

Beloved by Vancouverites, many of whom spend years exploring its hidden secrets, Stanley Park is truly the city's gift to the world. Located so close to downtown Vancouver that you feel you can reach out and touch the high rises, the park is a gateway into the two gentle solitudes of forest and sea.

The outer portion is circled by the Stanley Park seawall, which connects the park's recreational areas, while the interior of the park is overgrown and wild. For the most part, it is densely forested, with a network of bike and foot paths crisscrossing beneath fir and cedar boughs. Beaver Lake is a natural-state pond edged in cattails.

***Opposite top** Yachts moor near Stanley Park.
Opposite bottom Lumberman's Arch is a monument to the province's forestry history.
Above Beaches are another of Stanley Park's many attractions. **Bottom** Spring flowers come early to the park.*

35

Opposite *The Stanley Park seawall is a favourite of strollers and joggers.*
Above top *Great blue herons grace the shoreline.* **Bottom** *Siwash Rock, the source of Native legends.*

Construction on the 10.5-kilometre Stanley Park seawall began in 1917. To build the wall, huge slabs of granite were cut on the beach. Workers then dragged the blocks up to the wall, frequently working around the clock.

In spite of the relentless toil, the seawall took 63 years to complete.

Along the shoreline, Siwash Rock rises out of the ocean. This volcanic rock, a remnant of prehistoric times, is the source of many Native legends.

Nesting along the seawall near the Warren Harding Memorial, the great blue herons constantly arrive and depart throughout spring and early summer.

Aquarium

Located in Stanley Park, the Vancouver Aquarium is home to over 8000 species of aquatic life and provides a fascinating look into the underwater habitats of the Pacific Northwest coast and other underwater worlds.

The Vancouver Aquarium was Canada's first public aquarium. Opened in 1956, it has expanded to become the largest in Canada and one of the largest aquarium in North America. More than 800,000 people visit annually.

Whales, including friendly belugas and powerful killer whales, are the aquarium's major attraction. Attendants feed the killer whales several times a day. When the giant mammals are in the mood, they may leap high out of their new $10-million pool to astonish and delight viewers.

Four creative displays bring underwater environments to life. In the Pacific Northwest display, for example, playful sea otters busily clean their fur, octopus glide silently from crack to crevasse, and awe-inspiring killer whales watch you as closely as you watch them. In the North Pacific Habitat, scuba divers feed hungry halibut and harvest fast-growing kelp.

The creak of ice and the eerie language of whales dominate the Arctic Canada display. In this cold blue world, curious beluga whales are within touching distance.

In the aquarium's Amazon Rainforest, a steamy jungle with scarlet ibis and sleeping sloths is backdrop to the Giant Fishes of the Amazon display. In the Tropical Pacific Gallery, black-tipped reef sharks and stone fish simulate the diving experience from Hawaii to Australia. In the Indonesian Reef exhibit, a re-creation of that country's Bunaken National Marine Park

features hundreds of brilliantly coloured fish darting for cover in the reef.

The Vancouver Aquarium is internationally recognized for display and interpretation excellence and was the first facility to incorporate professional naturalists into the galleries to complement interpretive graphics. Aquarium research projects extend throughout the world, and the aquarium has successfully rehabilitated animals ranging from marine mammals to reptiles.

Opposite A beluga whale delights visitors in the Vancouver Aquarium's Arctic Canada Gallery. Above Haida artist Bill Reid's bronze sculpture, Killer Whale, *at the entrance to the aquarium. Bottom Killer whales, also known as orcas, are indigenous to the Pacific Northwest.*

University of BC

The second largest university in Canada and the oldest in British Columbia, the University of British Columbia (UBC) proves that institutions of higher learning needn't be dull and boring places. The campus includes public gardens and parks, theatres and museums, cafés and coffee shops, and one of the largest bookstores in Canada. An Olympic-size swimming pool is open to the public. Lectures, concerts, plays, art exhibits, and other displays attract year-round attention.

Serving over 100,000 full-time and part-time students every year, UBC boasts 12 faculties renowned for both scholarship and research.

Since its establishment in 1915, UBC has expanded its horizons to include the First Nations House of Learning and Longhouse.

After admiring the award-winning architecture of the longhouse, stroll over to the Institute of Asian Research, just steps away in the Asian Centre. UBC has one of the best Asian research collections in Canada. Directly behind the centre is the Nitobe Memorial Garden, a Japanese-style public garden.

With the spectacular Pacific Ocean as a backdrop, ancient times come to life here at the UBC Museum of Anthropology. Famed for its aboriginal studies and impressive collection of aboriginal art, the museum sits on the bluff of Point Grey, overlooking the Strait of Georgia. The museum's glass walls house a striking collection of Northwest Coast First Nations art and artifacts. Totem poles form one of the most memorable elements of the collection of more

than 12,000 archival objects. Carved by coastal artists from Haida, Tsimshian, Tlingit, Bella Coola, and Kwakiutl communities, the poles display family crest figures such as Raven, Bear, Killer Whale and Frog.

Opposite *The Museum of Anthropology pays homage to aboriginal cultures.* **Above** *Totem poles carved in British Columbia rest proudly on museum grounds with humans, animals and mythical beings represented.*

Gardens and Parks

No matter what time of year it is, Vancouver is a green and flowering city. With its moderate climate, plants may bloom year-round, surprising those recently arrived from more wintery climes. Whether you are driving or travelling on public transit, more than three dozen parks and gardens are easily accessible from downtown Vancouver.

Parks come in every size and shape. Stanley Park is undoubtedly the city's most famous, but others vie for attention. Pacific Spirit Regional Park, one of the newest, is close to the University of British Columbia (UBC). Covering 800 hectares (2000 acres), Pacific Spirit has 53 kilometres of walking, jogging, cycling and equestrian trails. Its leafy canopies and dense undergrowth exemplify the lushness of the West Coast rain forest.

Queen Elizabeth Park, one of the city's oldest, was established in 1912. Located on Little Mountain, the city's highest point, this well-groomed park offers an exceptional view of Vancouver.

The list of parks includes beach parks, mountain-side parks, lake parks, urban parks, and nature parks. Offering everything from rugged wilderness and hiking trails to moderate strolls.

Opposite Flowers bloom year-round in Queen Elizabeth Park. *Inset* Canada geese like to drop in and stay a while. *Above* An indoor garden, the Bloedel Floral Conservatory in Queen Elizabeth Park, houses 500 species of plants.

Queen Elizabeth Park rests on the highest point overlooking Vancouver's city centre. A peaceful respite
from the bustle of the city, the park's 53 hectares
(131 acres) feature flowering plants, trees, and bush-
es. Strolling along meandering walkways past foun-
tains and waterfalls, you're likely to come upon a wed-
ding party or two. The park's facilities include the
Bloedel Floral Conservatory, a gift shop, and the
Seasons in the Park Restaurant with its spectacular
view of the North Shore mountains.

S et against a panorama of city skyline and coastal mountains, the VanDusen Botanical Gardens are internationally known for their beautiful floral arrays.

An hour-long visit could be spent walking around the lakes or up in the Sino Himalayan Mountainscape. At any time you can visit the year-round displays of flowers and trees or dine in the gardens' Sprinklers Restaurant.

From mid-December to New Year's Day, the Festival of Lights takes place nightly. Twenty thousand twinkling lights adorn seasonal displays in this delightful winter celebration.

Over 6500 kinds of plants, assembled from six continents, grace the VanDusen Botanical Gardens. A highlight for children is the Elizabethan maze planted with 1000 pyramidal cedars.

Opposite Bear and man appear in Gitksan carver Arthur Sterritt's totem pole at the VanDusen Gardens. *Above* The foliage of the coastal rain forest is shown in this canopy. *Bottom* A wooden walkway in Pacific Spirit Regional Park.

The University of British Columbia is proud of its many public gardens. Its first, the UBC Botanical Garden, was introduced in 1916 on 2 hectares (5 acres) of land on a Point Grey site. By the early 1950s, gardens were spread out over the entire campus.

The David C. Lam Asian Garden, a 12-hectare (30-acre) forest garden, presents a rich variety of Asian plant life thriving harmoniously in a B.C. setting. The Physick Garden takes you time-travelling, stepping inside, you find yourself in a 16th-century monastery herb garden.

Yet another jewel-like space is the Nitobe Memorial Garden. This informal Japanese garden offers a variety of views from stopping points beside benches and on bridges. Waterfalls, rivers, forests, islands and seas, and even mountains are all presented in miniature.

Opposite *The passing of the seasons is reflected in the waters of the Nitobe Memorial Garden.* **Above** *Elegant great blue herons take flight.*

Above Flowering trees send winter
packing on Vancouver streets
Top left Spring arrives early at Kitsilano
Beach. **Bottom** New friends come in
every size and shape.

S even giant Douglas fir and western red cedars, known as the Seven Sisters, once towered over visitors in the early days of Stanley Park. The Hollow Tree, a giant red cedar 18 metres in girth, was another Stanley Park wonder. Street after street is festooned with Vancouver's annual spring celebration of colour. In all, there are more than 50,000 plum trees, 18,600 cherry trees, 1500 dogwood, 2900 flowering hawthorn, 1000 flowering pear, 1000 flowering ash, and 2600 chestnut trees lining the city's streets.

Beaches

Cross the Burrard Street Bridge and you leave the hustle of the city behind—until you get to Kitsilano Beach. Enroute, you'll pass the Vancouver Museum, Maritime Museum, and H.R. MacMillan Planetarium in Vanier Park. Leaving your car behind in the free parking lot, wander along the shore of English Bay to Kitsilano Beach, a five-minute walk away.

On a sunny day, this popular beach is packed with well-oiled bodies lazing about, playing volleyball, bicycling, swimming, and suntanning (the suntanning often starts in March). Some even rouse themselves to swim in the gentle waves that roll onto the beach.

If you'd prefer to swim in a pool, the Olympic-size Kitsilano Pool is a summer classic, open seven days a week. Small children are welcome, with a well-guarded shallow end set aside for their enjoyment. A Parks Board fish and chips stand feeds the hungry masses, and there are plenty of nearby restaurants and cafés for more genteel fare.

West of Kits Beach are four additional beaches: Jericho Beach and Jericho Park, Locarno Beach, Spanish Banks and Wreck Beach. Jericho, Locarno and Spanish Banks, are family beaches; Wreck Beach, is the city's unofficial nudist beach—reached by a long hike down the shoreline past Spanish Banks or down a steep wooded trail from UBC.

__Opposite top__ Kitsilano Pool combines sea water and sunshine. __Opposite bottom__ Front-row centre for Vancouver's annual bathtub race. __Above__ Bronzed bodies bask on Kitsilano Beach just minutes from downtown.

North Shore

The Lions Gate Bridge twinkles at night with thousands of lights, brightening the North Shore communities of West Vancouver and North Vancouver. The garlanded bridge lights the way to Grouse Mountain, Mount Seymour, and, farther up Howe Sound, Whistler and Blackcomb Mountains.

From the top of the Grouse Mountain gondola ride, you can gaze down 1120 metres to see Vancouver stretched out below. Like Grouse Mountain, Cypress Provincial Park offers winter skiing and summer hiking through meadows and forest. Another winter-summer area is Mount Seymour Provincial Park. Hikers, skiers, mountaineers and sightseers revel in the views from its many trails.

To savour the North Shore, the route from the Second Narrows Bridge to Horseshoe Bay along Marine Drive is highly recommended. After stopping at Lonsdale Quay, Marine Drive passes through Ambleside and Dundarave. Narrowing, it then weaves its way along the water's edge, past small pleasure craft hugging the shore or nestled in safe harbours. After a late lunch in Horseshoe Bay, return to Vancouver by way of the Lions Gate Bridge.

Opposite top The Grouse Mountain Skyride offers an unparalleled view. *Opposite bottom* Ski Grouse Mountain in the morning and sail English Bay in the afternoon. *Above* BC Transit's SeaBus crosses Vancouver Harbour.

Vancouver's oldest tourist attraction, the Capilano Suspension Bridge and Park, draws over half a million visitors each year. Built in 1889, the suspension footbridge is the world's longest and highest, measuring 137 metres across and swinging 70 metres above the Capilano River.
Inset Daring visitors cross into the park by way of the gently swaying steel cable footbridge, floored with cedar planks. Just minutes from downtown Vancouver, the park is set in the West Coast rain forest. Preserved in its natural state, the 9-hectare (22-acre) historic site includes wooded trails, tranquil trout ponds, and towering evergreens.

In the 1860s, 70 years after European explorers had visited the Coast Salish people in Burrard Inlet, the finest stands of timber on the coast brought settlers, industry, and waterfront activity to the North Shore. Trees grew 100 metres or more, straight and knot-free. The massive cedar beams from the Lower Mainland can actually be seen in the ceilings of the Imperial Palace in Beijing.

Lonsdale Quay, in North Vancouver, is a major retail centre, complete with market, hotel, and entertainment complex. Created as part of a multi-million-dollar waterfront refurbishment project, the quay is right on the waterfront at the SeaBus terminal.

In 1986, the Lonsdale Quay Market opened its doors. The public market sells fresh fruit and vegetables, meat, and seafood, and specialty shops offer everything from French pastries to magazines to fine jewellery and fashions. The Lower Lonsdale area of North Vancouver is also the site of an unprecedented number of high-rise developments.

Opposite Lonsdale Quay is a 15-minute SeaBus ride from downtown Vancouver. *Above* A North Shore view of the Vancouver skyline at night, with Grouse Mountain sparkling above the city.

In West Vancouver's Lighthouse Park, a traditional beacon of safe harbour stands on guard overlooking the Strait of Georgia.

Marine Drive snakes along the coast to West Vancouver's inviting village of Horseshoe Bay. The route meanders past sleepy marinas and cliff-hugging residences, owned by some of the North Shore's wealthiest citizens.

Horseshoe Bay was once known to its Native inhabitants as Chai-hai, meaning a low sizzling noise—probably made by small fish jumping along the shore in the evening. Today a more likely sound is the hoot of a BC Ferry enroute to Vancouver Island, the Sunshine Coast or Bowen Island.

In spite of progress, Horseshoe Bay retains much of its original charm. With a population of just over 1000 people tucked into the surrounding hills, this once little-known summer hideaway maintains a community feeling.

***Opposite** Secluded bays add pleasure to sailing, a popular pastime on the coast. **Above** Marine Drive hugs the shoreline. **Bottom** Ferries leave Horseshoe Bay daily for Nanaimo, the Sunshine Coast and Bowen Island.*

An estimated 20,000 people now live in "Sea to Sky Country," which extends from Horseshoe Bay northward to Whistler, the province's highly acclaimed winter and summer resort.

There are many ways to head north on Highway 99 to Whistler. Unquestionably, the most picturesque journey is by way of BC Rail's Royal Hudson, the last steam locomotive still in service in Canada. As the Royal Hudson steams up Howe Sound, its throaty whistle has been described as "the sound of summer."

The Royal Hudson, built for fast passenger service by Montreal Locomotive Works for the Canadian Pacific Railway (CPR), took its first trip in 1940. Early on in its career, the Royal Hudson pulled transcontinental passenger trains between Revelstoke and Vancouver. A serious derailment in 1956 along Vancouver's Burrard Inlet, however, led many to believe that the locomotive was beyond repair. A timely reprieve resulted in its refurbishment. After further duty in Winnipeg, the Royal Hudson seemed destined to be replaced by more modern methods of travel. Finally acquired by the Province of British Columbia in 1973, the steam giant was lovingly restored to operating perfection. Its inaugural run from North Vancouver to Squamish was made on June 20, 1974. Wearing the Coat of Arms of the Province of British Columbia, the locomotive serves as a legacy to the age of steam travel.

Passing over trestles and through six tunnels, the Royal Hudson has now travelled the 64-kilometre North Vancouver-Squamish line more than 2000 times. Passengers do not have to be steam enthusiasts to enjoy one of the province's most popular tourist attractions and to appreciate the majesty of this proud engine.

Above *The Royal Hudson, the last steam locomotive in service in Canada, carries passengers along scenic Howe Sound.*